M000211200

HOUGHTON MIFFLIN

Reading

A Legacy of Literacy

Animal
Encounters

HOUGHTON MIFFLIN   BOSTON · MORRIS PLAINS, NJ

California · Colorado · Georgia · Illinois · New Jersey · Texas

Design, Art Management and Page Production: Kirchoff/Wohlberg, Inc.

ILLUSTRATION CREDITS
4, 6-10, 13-14, 16-17, 19-20, 23 Eileen Hine. **26-30. 32, 34. 36, 38, 40, 42, 44, 46, 47** Tom Leonard. **48-69** Patrick Faricy.

PHOTOGRAPHY CREDITS
4 Jerry Lesser. **5** Jerry Lesser. **6-7** Jerry Lesser. **8-9** Robert Gill/Corbis. **8** (t) Peter Davey/Bruce Coleman, Inc. **9** (t) Hughes/Bruce Coleman, Inc. **10** Jerry Lesser. **11** Jerry Lesser. **12-3** Jerry Lesser. **14-5** Jerry Lesser. **16** Jerry Lesser. **17** Jerry Lesser. **18** Jerry Lesser. **19** Jerry Lesser. **20** Jerry Lesser. **21** Jerry Lesser. **22-3** Tom Nebbia/Corbis. **23** (t) Jerry Lesser. **24** Jerry Lesser. **25** Jerry Lesser. **26** (bkgd) Danny Lehman/Corbis. **26** (i) Lynda Richardson/Corbis. **29** Doug Perrine/DRK Photo. **30-1** Erwin & Peggy Bauer/Bruce Coleman, Inc. **32** Jeff Simon/Bruce Coleman, Inc. **33** Fred Bruemmer/DRK Photo. **34-5** Krasemann/Photo Researchers. **35** (i) Stoy/Bruce Coleman, Inc. **36** (l) Dave G. Houser/Corbis. **36-7** Jeremy Horner/Corbis. **37** (t) Herb Segars/Animals Animals. **38** Craig Lovell/Corbis. **38** (i) Lynda Richardson/Corbis. **39** CC Lockwood/Animals Animals. **40** Robert Pickett/Corbis. **41** Jeffrey Rotman/Corbis. **42** Doug Wechsler/Animals Animals. **43** Nik Wheeler/Corbis. **44-5** Jeff Simon/Bruce Coleman, Inc. **45** (t) Fred Whitehead/Animals Animals. **46** CC Lockwood/Bruce Coleman, Inc. **47** (t) Danny Lehman/Corbis. **47** (b) Kevin Schafer/Corbis.

Printed in U.S.A.

ISBN: 0-618-04412-4

10 11 12 13 14 - VH - 06 05 04 03

Animal
Encounters

Contents

The
HYRAX
of
Top-Knot Island

by Robin Bernard

photography by
Jerry Lesser

Strategy Focus

Have you ever seen a hyrax? As you read
about hyraxes, **evaluate** how the author tells
you about them and where they live.

4

You can't smell the ocean from Top-Knot Island, or hear the splash of waves or the cries of gulls. That's because this rocky island isn't like any other island you've ever seen. It's right in the middle of a sea of grass, on the flat plains of Africa.

Top-Knot Island is really a group of boulders known as a "kopje." Like a real island, it has its own climate, plants, and animals. I went there to study one of those animals, one that most people have never heard of. It's called the hyrax.

I saw my first hyrax on an earlier trip to Africa. I had climbed some rocks to take pictures of lizards. After a while, I got the feeling I was being watched.

Sure enough, there was a furry little creature looking at me. As soon as I snapped its picture, it ran away.

A moment later it was back. This time it brought along some friends. They all lined up to stare at the two-legged animal with the camera. Maybe it was their funny smiles or bright eyes, but something made me want to find out more about them.

Hyraxes aren't well-known animals. In fact, many people have never heard of them. Maybe that's because hyraxes don't look or act as special as some other animals. Hyraxes don't have graceful horns or beautiful fur. They don't roar or run like the wind. At first glance, they look a lot like big guinea pigs.

Yet to scientists, the hyrax is a very interesting puzzle. Its stomach is like a horse's. Some of its teeth are like a hippo's, some are like a rhino's, and some are like a rodent's.

But if you ask scientists to name the hyrax's closest relative, they will tell you it's the elephant. Clearly, hyraxes don't look anything like elephants. But their front leg bones, feet, and brains are a lot like an elephant's.

Hyraxes and elephants are also alike in other ways. Most mammals that are as small as hyraxes give birth to their babies in about eight weeks. But a hyrax mother needs seven and a half months to have babies. An elephant mother also takes a long time to give birth.

PETER DAVEY

CAROL HUGHES

Hyraxes and elephants have something else in common, too. They both have trouble cooling down.

Elephants can dunk themselves in a river or pond. They can also flap their ears to cool off.

Hyraxes try to keep cool by living on a kopje. If they get too warm, they can go into the shady spaces between the rocks. Top-Knot even has a cave where the air never gets too warm.

But hyraxes have more to worry about than elephants do. That's because hyraxes are small enough to make an easy meal, while elephants are not.

So hyraxes always keep an eye out for danger. There's often a hyrax standing guard on one of the kopje's highest boulders. From there he can spot a hungry eagle a mile away. He also watches the grass for prowling leopards, who are very fond of hyrax "snacks."

If the hyrax guard sees anything dangerous, he gives a high whistle. The alarm sends the whole hyrax colony diving into the deep, dark spaces between the rocks. In seconds, there's not a hyrax to be seen.

The kopje offers more than protection to the hyrax. It offers something else that's just as important — food.

In Africa's dry season, the sun beats down and there is very little rain. The grass that covers the plains often turns brown and dies. But green plants almost always grow on Top-Knot. Morning dew collects on the rocks and then trickles into the soil. Then it's soaked up by plant roots.

op-Knot's green plants attract many fur-covered and feather-covered visitors.

One morning while I was watching the hyraxes eat their breakfast, I saw two giraffes picking their way along the lower rocks of the kopje. The hyraxes seemed as surprised as I was to see the giraffes there.

The giraffes stretched their long legs and long necks and stuck out their long tongues, but they still couldn't reach the leaves they wanted. After a while, the giraffes gave up and went off. All of Top-Knot's greenery is easy for hyraxes to reach, because they can scamper up and down the rocks.

After the giraffes left, the hyraxes kept munching away on their morning meal. A few minutes later, I heard squeaks and squeals right below me. Pygmy mongooses! They wiggled, jumped, and rolled over. Finally, one stopped long enough for me to take its picture.

Just knowing these snake-killers lived on the kopje made me feel safer. I hadn't met a deadly snake yet, and I hoped I never would. Their poison can kill someone almost instantly.

The next day, three tiny hyraxes appeared at the kopje. They looked more like puppies than African wild animals. I didn't spot their mother right away, but I knew she must be nearby. Aha! There she was, on a ledge just a few yards away, watching every move her babies made.

The cubs inched closer and closer to me. They came so near I could almost reach out and touch them. Just then, their mom decided they were getting too nosy. She gave a soft call, and immediately the cubs ran back to her side.

It was a good thing she called them. I knew that people should never touch wild animals, but those fluffy cubs were very hard to resist.

During the summer I spent studying the hyraxes, I found out a lot about their habits. For one thing, I learned how some hyrax cubs get so good at climbing rocks. They practice by jumping onto their mothers. Then they may climb up her back and reach her neck. Finally, they may get all the way up to the top of her head.

I saw one cub hop onto his mother's back many times every day. He jumped up easily, but getting down was another matter. Each time he jumped off his mom, he got better at it. In a few more days, he became very good at climbing on hyraxes. Then he was able to climb up and down the rocks easily.

The hyraxes grew used to having me around. If I just sat quietly, they nibbled flowers and leaves right near me. One day, when a female hyrax came very close to me, I saw something I hadn't noticed before. She had a few long hairs evenly spaced along her back. They were stiff, just like a cat's whiskers. Later, I found out that the hairs are used as "feelers." In caves and dark spaces between the rocks, these special hairs are like extra hands that help hyraxes "feel" where to go.

Like most mammals, hyrax cubs greet each other by sniffing. I watched them do this over and over again. After sniffing, one hyrax ran a short way off and looked back at me. It seemed to be asking, "Are you ready to play?" Cubs often go nose to nose with adult hyraxes, too. The grown-ups nuzzle them for a moment, and then give them a gentle shove toward their playmates.

Adult hyraxes hardly ever sniff each other face to face. If they do, they usually end up fighting.

The adults spend most of their time fanned out or resting back to back. Lying that way helps the hyraxes in two ways. First of all, it helps prevent fights, because the hyraxes are facing away from each other. Second, facing out means they can see in many directions. That gives the hyraxes a better chance of spotting any enemies.

During the midday heat, hyraxes rest in their cool dens. When I was watching them, I took my lunch break while they rested. But one afternoon it looked as if lunch would have to wait a while. Standing at the foot of Top-Knot was a handsome, very large rhino! He was so close, I could see every fringe on his ears. Luckily, he didn't notice me.

When the rhino finally left, I climbed down to my car to get my lunch. Just as I finished eating, I thought I saw something move in a thorn tree. I looked more closely. I found a pair of yellow eyes staring back at me.

It seems that I wasn't the only one eager to see the hyraxes again. A long, lean leopard was stretched out on a nearby tree limb. He waited and watched. He looked as if he was ready for a hyrax snack.

The hyraxes slowly came out of their resting places. As they did, the leopard slowly climbed down the tree. It started moving very quietly toward the kopje. I held my breath.

Suddenly, one of the old male hyraxes sounded the alarm. At almost the same moment, a herd of impalas ran across the grassy plains. The leopard glanced at the kopje once more and then turned and ran after the impalas. After all, impalas were big enough for a feast, not just a snack. I gave a big sigh of relief.

When it started getting dark, I walked back to my car and climbed inside. Just then, two hyrax cubs hopped on the roof. They peeked in at me, and then they jumped off. They ran back to the kopje to play tag on the rocks.

As I drove away, I thought about their narrow escape from the leopard. But I figured those cubs would probably survive most dangers. All the things that make hyraxes easy to overlook add to their safety. Their small size and gray-brown fur help them blend in with their background. They have few enemies, and people don't hunt them for food or for their fur. And best of all, hyraxes have the perfect home.

Before I knew it, my summer at the kopje was over. When I had arrived, I was only interested in hyraxes. By the time I left, everything on and around Top-Knot Island was special to me. The kopje had become far more than a heap of rocks. It was home for some wonderful creatures, and it offered food to many others as well. But the hyrax would always be my favorite of all the animals I had seen.

I left at sunset. As I drove away, I stole a last look at Top-Knot and said a silent goodbye.

Responding

Think About the Selection

1. What makes Top-Knot Island different from other islands?

2. Why do you think the author was able to learn so much about the hyraxes and other animals?

3. Why is Top-Knot Island perfect for hyraxes?

Making Generalizations

Several facts can support a single generalization. Copy the web on a piece of paper. Then write information from the story that supports the generalization.

```
┌─────────┐           ┌─────────┐
│    ?    │           │    ?    │
└─────────┘           └─────────┘
        ┌──────────────────┐
        │  GENERALIZATION  │
        │ Hyraxes always keep an │
        │  eye out for danger.   │
        └──────────────────┘
┌──────────────────┐   ┌─────────┐
│ There's often a hyrax │ │    ?    │
│   standing guard.     │ └─────────┘
└──────────────────┘
```

Saving Sea Turtles

by Amy Edgar   illustrated by Tom Leonard

Strategy Focus

Will sea turtles disappear? As you read the story, stop now and then to **monitor** how well you understand the turtles' problems, and reread to **clarify**.

INTRODUCING SEA TURTLES

Sea turtles have lived on Earth since the days of the dinosaurs. Scientists think they may be related to crocodiles and even birds.

Three Kinds of Sea Turtles

Hawksbill   **Kemp's Ridley**   **Loggerhead**

There are seven kinds of sea turtles. All of them are endangered. The Kemp's Ridley sea turtle is the closest to extinction. In 1947, 40,000 Kemp's Ridley sea turtles laid eggs on a single day. In 1998, only 2,000 of them laid eggs in an entire year.

Why are there so few left today? One answer is that we have harmed both the turtles and their natural habitat. Scientists are afraid that Kemp's Ridley sea turtles might soon disappear from the oceans forever.

FEATURES OF SEA TURTLES

Sea turtles are like land turtles in some ways. They are also quite different. A land turtle can pull its head inside its shell to hide from danger. A sea turtle cannot. Instead, it swims away from danger. A land turtle has feet and claws for walking. A sea turtle has flippers for swimming.

land turtle

Kemp's Ridley

Sea turtles are the fastest swimmers of all animals with four legs. Some have been recorded swimming as fast as 20 miles per hour. A sea turtle's flippers are shaped like paddles. It swims by moving its two front flippers — like a bird flapping its wings. At the same time, it steers with its back flippers. No one knows for sure how deep sea turtles go when they dive and swim.

A Kemp's Ridley sea turtle is smaller than other sea turtles. It is about two feet long with a dark green-gray shell and skin. The average weight of a Kemp's Ridley sea turtle is 100 pounds. The average weight of a Leatherback sea turtle is 1,000 pounds.

Leatherback

Kemp's Ridley

Sea turtles need to breathe air. Their lungs remove every bit of oxygen from the air that they breathe. That way they can stay underwater for a long time. Active turtles swim to the surface for a breath every few minutes. Resting turtles can stay underwater for up to two hours. When it is time for a turtle to sleep, it sinks to the bottom of the ocean. There the water is colder and less oxygen is needed to breathe.

A sea turtle never chews its food, because it doesn't have any teeth. Instead, it crushes its prey with its powerful jaws. Its jaws are so strong that it can crush just about anything, even tough clam shells. A Kemp's Ridley sea turtle eats mostly fish and shellfish. Two of its favorite foods are crabs and jellyfish.

A sea turtle lives its life alone in the ocean. Only the female sea turtle ever returns to land. Here's what happens when a Kemp's Ridley sea turtle returns to lay her eggs.

A SEA TURTLE RETURNS TO LAND

The scene is a windswept beach on Padre Island, Texas. A Kemp's Ridley sea turtle struggles onto the shore. She hasn't been on land since she was a baby turtle, a hatchling.

The sea turtle is graceful and speedy in the water, but she is clumsy and slow on land. She drags herself over the sand with her flippers. Soon she reaches a part of the beach that is safely above the high tide mark. Using her back flippers, she begins to dig a hole in the sand.

When the hole is deep enough, the sea turtle starts to lay her eggs. One after another, the soft, round eggs drop into the hole. They look a little like Ping-Pong balls. When she finishes, she covers them with sand. Then she slowly makes her way back to the water and swims out to sea.

Her eggs will hatch in about fifty days, but she won't be around to greet her babies. Turtle babies aren't like human babies. They don't need their parents' help to survive. They are born knowing how to find their way into the ocean. They are also born knowing how to swim. But they have to struggle to stay alive.

THE STRUGGLE TO SURVIVE

The survival of sea turtles is threatened by humans in many different ways. Shrimp boats drag huge nets to catch shrimp. Some sea turtles also get caught in the nets. Sea turtles are hunted for their skin, shells, and meat. Wallets, jewelry, and soup made from sea turtles are still being sold in some parts of the world.

People living near beaches are also a threat to the survival of sea turtles. Humans can crush sea turtle eggs by accident as they play at the beach. Pollution also kills sea turtles. They often swallow things like plastic bags. The bags may look like jellyfish to the turtles. The plastic can choke them. Or it can keep them floating at the surface of the water, unable to dive for food.

PROTECTING SEA TURTLES

Some people are concerned about the fate of sea turtles. They are taking action to save them. A Turtle Excluding Device (TED) was invented so that people can fish for shrimp without trapping turtles. The TED lets turtles escape the fisherman's net. Sadly, many people are not willing to use TEDs when they fish for shrimp.

They say the TEDs cost much
more than regular nets and are
harder to use.

Others are doing their
best to help turtles that nest on
beaches where many people go.
A hotel in Palm Beach, Florida,
has a boardwalk that leads to
the beach. It helps prevent
guests from disturbing the eggs
that may be buried there.

SCIENTISTS STEP IN

Some scientists and volunteers help to protect sea turtle eggs. They also protect the baby turtles when they hatch.

First, a volunteer spots turtle tracks leading down to the water. Those tracks show that a female sea turtle has left her eggs nearby. The volunteer beeps the scientist who is on duty. Then the volunteer watches the area around the turtle tracks until the scientist arrives. As he watches, a gust of wind might come along and blow away the turtle tracks. But because the volunteer has been watching closely, the scientist can still find the eggs when he gets there.

DO NOT REMOVE
SEA TURTLE NEST
VIOLATORS SUBJECT TO FINES AND IMPRISONMENT

Soon the scientist arrives to dig up the turtle eggs. He counts them. Then he carefully places them in a box. He also puts some sand from the nesting site into the box. He hopes that burying the eggs in that sand will help the turtles come back to the same beach when they are adults.

In his notebook the scientist writes down the number of eggs, how deep the nest is, the time of day, and the weather. Then he marks the nesting site with a pole. He will return to it with the baby turtles when they are ready to be released into the ocean.

AT THE LABORATORY

Back at the science laboratory, the eggs are gently buried in a hole just like the one the mother turtle dug for them. Then the waiting begins. It will be about fifty days before the baby turtles begin to hatch. The scientist will watch over the eggs, making sure that they don't get too hot or too cold.

Finally, the turtles start hatching and moving about
in the nesting hole. The hatchlings work together to dig
their way out of the sand.

The scientist counts and weighs the baby turtles.
Then he calls volunteers and tells them to meet him at the
beach where they discovered and collected the eggs.

BACK ON THE BEACH

On the beach, volunteers stand near the shore. They guard the baby sea turtles as they crawl out of the box. Two boys chase away some sea gulls and a crab that might have harmed the hatchlings. One baby sea turtle begins to go the wrong way, away from the ocean. A girl picks it up and gently places it in the water. In a flash, it swims off to its new life in the ocean.

That life will be a hard one. Baby sea turtles have many enemies in the ocean. They may be eaten by a large fish or crab, swallow the plastic top from a juice container that was carelessly tossed away, or drown in a net. Scientists believe that only 1 out of 100 hatchlings survives to be an adult turtle.

WHAT WILL HAPPEN TO THE KEMP'S RIDLEY SEA TURTLE?

Scientists hope that protecting the hatching and release of Kemp's Ridley sea turtles will help their numbers to grow. They also hope the hatchling turtles will return to Padre Island to nest when they are adults. Whether this will happen or not is still a mystery.

For now, the Kemp's Ridley sea turtle is still in serious danger. However, there is reason for hope. Over the last five years, the number of nests counted in Mexico and Texas has gone up. In 1995 only four nests were found on Padre Island. In 1998, 13 were found.

Can a creature that outlived the dinosaurs survive in our world? Only time will tell.

THINK ABOUT THE SELECTION

1 What kind of sea turtle is most likely to disappear?

2 What has hurt the Kemp's Ridley sea turtle?

3 What is the main idea of this story? (Reread page 45.)

TOPIC, MAIN IDEAS, AND SUPPORTING DETAILS

Copy the chart on a piece of paper. Fill in the topic, one main idea, and a supporting detail for each main idea.

Topic: _____ ? _____

Main Ideas	Supporting Details
?	• A land turtle can pull its head in, but a sea turtle can't. • ?
People are trying to save sea turtles.	• Scientists and volunteers protect sea turtle eggs. • ?

KAT
THE CURIOUS

by Barbara Brook Simons
illustrations by Patrick Faricy

Strategy Focus

Where will Kat's curiosity lead her? As you read, stop at important points in the story to **summarize** what has happened.

I didn't plan to get lost. Actually, I was never *really* lost. I was just — you know, curious. I'm sorry I scared everyone, though. I guess the only person who wasn't scared was me! Here's what happened.

I was going to spend a week with Aunt Helen
while my parents went camping in the Rocky
Mountains. I should tell you that Helen is not my *real*
aunt. She's an old friend of my mother's, and since she
has no children of her own, she's kind of adopted me
as her niece. She has a little log cabin on a hilltop in
the woods, with a big stone chimney and a great view.

The cabin is only about forty miles from a city, but it feels farther away than that. I guess that's because Aunt Helen has no electricity or phone line. We use kerosene lamps and candles. (Aunt Helen does bring her cell phone for emergencies — she's not *that* much of a pioneer.)

My parents and I left home very early that morning, and we got to the cabin at about 2:30. Aunt Helen expected us at around three, so we were a little early. Sure enough, she wasn't home. (Aunt Helen is hardly *ever* home unless she has to be.)

Hi folks!
In case you get here
early, I've gone to town
for some of that cheddar
cheese that Kat likes.
I'll be back before three.

Anyway, there was a note on the door that said, "Hi, folks! In case you get here early, I've gone to town for some of that cheddar cheese that Kat likes. I'll be back before three."

I saw my dad looking at his watch. "Why don't you guys take off?" I said. "I'll be fine, and Helen will be back soon. And if I really want to get in, I know how to go through the kitchen window. Don't worry about me. Have a great time!"

I must have been pretty convincing. After many good-bye hugs, they left.

I sat on the porch steps. The air smelled of warm grass and sweet clover. The last thing I wanted was to be inside. I just wanted to sit and listen to the sounds of nature. After all, I'd been listening to city noises all year. (Talk about ear pollution . . . !)

A warm breeze rustled the tops of the trees, and grasshoppers chirped in the tall, purple-flowered weeds. A loud "rat-tat-tat" told me that a woodpecker was drumming on a nearby tree.

Suddenly I heard a rustling noise behind the cabin, where Helen kept the garbage can. Maybe a raccoon was looking for a snack.

That reminded me that I was hungry. I was unwrapping a sandwich when a chipmunk ran along the porch railing. It stopped and flicked its tail, and I gave it a bit of sandwich.

After I finished eating, I began to get impatient. Where *was* Aunt Helen? I'd come all this way to enjoy the woods, and I couldn't wait any longer. I was dying to see my favorite places again.

I saw a flash of color in the trees and said, "What *is* that bird?" That's when I knew I had to go explore — right now. I knew these woods very well and was certain I could find my way.

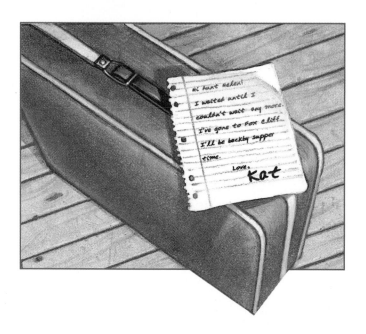

I wrote a note on a page from my notebook.
It said, "Hi Aunt Helen! I waited until I couldn't wait
anymore. I've gone to Fox Cliff. I'll be back by
suppertime. Love, Kat."

I put the note on top of my suitcase. Then I put
on my backpack and walked into the shady woods.

Under the trees, the air was cool and fresh. As I
headed for Fox Cliff, sunlight shone through the
leaves, making small, dancing patterns on the ground.
I should mention that Fox Cliff is a bluff of carved
sandstone near the river. I'd been there a hundred
times. Well, maybe more like nine or ten times, to be
truthful.

Acorns crunched on the path under my feet. The noise startled two squirrels, who jumped to a branch over my head. I tossed bits of peanut butter cookie toward them. They ran down the tree and scampered off with the crumbs. Then they followed me, hoping they'd get some more.

They kept up with me as the trail twisted and turned. When I passed a huge hollow tree, they jumped into it and watched me go on my way.

I continued on the trail, making all the turns I remembered. Pretty soon, I thought, the path would wind uphill. Then the woods would open out, and I'd be at the cliff. "Funny," I said to myself. "I didn't remember it was this far. I've been walking for a long time."

Suddenly, nothing looked familiar. I came to another fork in the path and knew that I had no idea which way to go.

I chose one path and started down it. I was really lost. The trees' shadows were getting longer, and my watch said it was getting late. I couldn't possibly get back to the cabin in the dark — even if I knew the way.

It was then that I realized I would have to spend the night in the woods. I wasn't really worried. In fact, I thought it was kind of exciting. But I knew Aunt Helen would be out of her mind with worry, and I felt bad about that.

I looked in my backpack. I had a little food—half a sandwich, an apple, and some chips—a flashlight, and a knife. I had warm clothes, too. What I needed was fresh water. A little more to eat would be nice, but it wasn't necessary.

Something moved in the bushes. I sat very still while a raccoon with something in his mouth scurried past. I remembered that raccoons wash their food, so I scurried after it. He led me right to a spring bubbling out of a crack in a rock.

As I filled my water bottle, I looked at the shallow water at the edge of the stream. A bright green plant was growing there. Watercress! I picked handfuls of the spicy leaves for a wild salad.

The raccoon had already finished his dinner. He didn't seem to be afraid of me at all. He looked up at me through his black mask.

"Okay, Bandit," I said. The name just seemed to fit. "What do you eat that I can eat?" He trotted up the bank to a tangle of bushes loaded with small reddish fruit—wild plums. Bandit was inviting me over to his place for dessert!

Soon it was time to make camp. I'd had a long day, and I was awfully tired. I searched for a rocky overhang to lie under. That way, if it rained the overhang would keep me dry. Then I used my knife to cut some long green saplings, and I propped them against the rocks. I wove in thin branches to make a framework, and I draped my sweatshirt over it, making a kind of tent.

It was getting pretty dark. I wasn't scared —not really, anyway. There aren't any dangerous animals like bears or wolves in southern Wisconsin. I had a flashlight, but a fire would be nicer. "Wait a minute," I said to myself. "I took this backpack the last time I went camping. Maybe I still have that tin of matches." I did—six precious matches. I had to use two of them to light a fire.

The glow from the fire danced on the rocks behind me. Spring peepers cheeped in the trees. Big frogs rumbled in their bass voices.

I curled up on a bed of soft, dry grass and sweet-smelling pine needles. My extra sweater made a pretty good blanket. I watched the stars until I fell asleep.

The next morning I woke up early, with a squirrel scolding me. "Sorry, the peanut butter cookies are all gone," I said. "It's your turn to get breakfast. How about some nuts? Fruit? Cornflakes?" The squirrel ran up a hill toward some small trees. Round brown nuts hung from the branches.

"Hazelnuts!" I said. I'd never seen them growing before. Somewhere I'd read that the Winnebago Indians loved hazelnuts. Before they get ripe, the nuts are supposed to be soft and sweet. I smashed a shell, tried one, and found that it was true.

When I'd had my fill, I looked around. Through the oak trees, I saw the shape of a house! I climbed through spiky bushes toward it. When I got close, I saw that the house was a ruin with only one wall. Wild grapevines twisted over it.

I was nibbling some grapes when Bandit poked his nose around the corner. "Do you want some grapes, Bandit?" I asked, as I put a few on the ground. He picked them up with his paws, which looked just like little hands. "You like people food, don't you, Bandit? Was that you in Aunt Helen's garbage can yesterday?"

Did Bandit understand me? I'll never know. Maybe he just knew that this was his world, and I didn't belong in it. In any case, he started off through the woods. It looked as if I should follow him, so I did.

Following Bandit, I saw how lost I was. I was nowhere near Fox Cliff. If people were looking there, they wouldn't find me. Bandit trotted quickly through the woods. I could see a faint path, not one made by people. Maybe it was the path that deer and other animals made when they went to the stream.

We went on that way for at least an hour. Then things began to look familiar. Suddenly, we came out of the woods—and there was Aunt Helen's cabin only a few yards away. Bandit scurried around the corner to the garbage can.

Aunt Helen was on the porch. When she saw me, she started to cry. "You're safe, you're safe! The state police are looking all over Fox Cliff! Why did you wander off like that? I must have gotten home just minutes after you left."

"I was just curious," I said. "I thought I knew the way. I'm really sorry I worried everybody."

"Kat the Curious," Aunt Helen said. "No more exploring on your own! Next time you get curious, I'm coming with you! Now what is that raccoon doing on the porch?"

Responding

Think About the Selection

1 Why does Kat get lost?

2 How does Kat take care of herself?

3 What conclusion does Kat come to that helps get her back to Helen's cabin?

Use Clues – Drawing Conclusions

One way to think about drawing conclusions is to keep a chart like this. Copy the chart on a piece of paper. Then complete the chart.

What Kat Knows	Kat's Conclusions
Kat knows raccoons wash their food.	If she follows a raccoon, it will lead her to water.
She can eat the same kind of food as a raccoon eats.	?
Squirrels know where to get nuts.	?